Official Mensa
Puzzle Book

clever crosswords

for kids

Trip Payne

D0003741

Sterling Publishing Co., Inc.
New York

Dedicated to Brian Dominy,
a grown-up who still remembers how much
fun it can be to act like a kid sometimes.

Other books by Trip Payne:

Crosswords for Kids
Great Crosswords for Kids
Super Crosswords for Kids
Challenging Crosswords for Kids
365 Celebrity Crypto-Quotes
Mighty Mini Crosswords
Crosswords to Strain Your Brain
The Little Giant® Encyclopedia of Word Puzzles (coauthor)

Mensa and the distinctive table logo are trademarks of
American Mensa, Ltd. (in the U.S.), British Mensa, Ltd. (in the U.K.),
and Mensa International Limited, Ltd. (in other countries)
and are used by permission.

8   10   9   7

Published by Sterling Publishing Co., Inc.
387 Park Avenue South, New York, NY 10016
© 2004 by Trip Payne
Distributed in Canada by Sterling Publishing
c/o Canadian Manda Group, 165 Dufferin Street,
Toronto, Ontario, Canada M6K 3H6
Distributed in Great Britain and Europe by Chris Lloyd at Orca Book
Services, Stanley House, Fleets Lane, Poole BH15 3AJ, England
Distributed in Australia by Capricorn Link (Australia) Pty. Ltd.
P.O. Box 704, Windsor, NSW 2756, Australia

Sterling ISBN-13: 978-1-4027-0556-4
ISBN-10: 1-4027-0556-5

For information about custom editions, special sales, premium and
corporate purchases, please contact Sterling Special Sales
Department at 800-805-5489 or specialsales@sterlingpub.com.

CONTENTS

INTRODUCTION

Crossword puzzles are fun.

See, they're not like homework. You can do them whenever you want, wherever you want, for however long you want.

You can solve them by yourself. You can solve them with someone else. You can ask someone for help when there's something you're not sure about. You can even peek at the answers if no one is looking!

There's no wrong way to solve a crossword. As long as you're having fun doing it, that's the right way to do it.

So, whenever you're ready, turn the page and start solving. And have fun!

—Trip Payne

PUZZLES

1

ACROSS

1 Fifty-yard ___ (kind of race)
5 Sick
8 Money that's given to a waiter
11 State that borders Indiana
12 Large body of water
13 Twelve minus eleven
14 Phrase shouted on January 1: 3 words
17 Give someone a ___ on the back
18 What the French word "oui" means in English
19 Capital of Oregon
22 Animal that's housebroken
23 A baseball player uses one
26 Like hand-me-downs
27 Moe runs one on "The Simpsons"
28 What a barber cuts
29 Old, broken-down horse
30 Lacking water
31 Very tired
32 Burned ___ crisp: 2 words
33 Brown drink
34 Phrase shouted on October 31: 3 words
40 Meat that comes from pigs
41 Female sheep
42 Mexican food
43 Place for a contact lens
44 "Monkey ___, monkey do"
45 Beef ___ (hearty meal)

DOWN

1 Play-___ (material similar to clay)
2 "Now I get it!"
3 Small drink
4 Moved like a rabbit
5 "It ___ fair!"
6 Sara ___ (brand of frozen desserts)
7 Attorney
8 You have ten of them on your body
9 "Four-and-twenty blackbirds baked ___ pie": 2 words
10 Miles ___ hour
15 Vegetable similar to a sweet potato

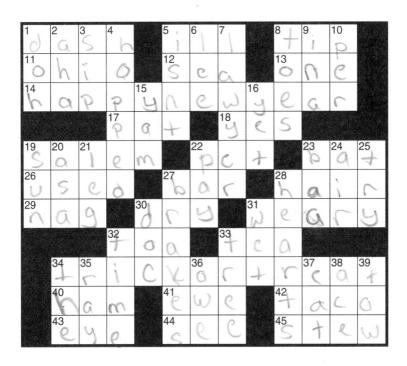

16 "Are we there ___?"

19 The planets revolve around it

20 Fit ___ fiddle: 2 words

21 Chicken drumstick

22 Spend money

23 What a lamb says

24 ___ conditioning

25 Attempt

27 Pedals that stop cars

28 A red suit, in cards

30 One of the Seven Dwarfs

31 Moist

32 For the ___ being (for now)

33 Apple or maple, for example

34 "Beauty and ___ Beast"

35 X-___ vision (one of Superman's powers)

36 What the O stands for in "I.O.U."

37 Devour

38 High card

39 Rescue a car

2

ACROSS

1 Buddy
4 Insects that like picnics
8 Green ___ Packers (pro football team)
11 Put ___ fight: 2 words
12 Part of a finger
13 "You ___ what you eat"
14 Popular brand of cookies: 2 words
17 "___-hoo!" (what you say to get someone's attention)
18 Christmas ___ (December 24)
19 Stuff in a museum
22 "Don't put all your eggs in ___ basket"
24 The King of rock and roll
28 The first word of a letter
30 Kind of tree
32 Walk back and forth
33 You pour it over pancakes
35 It can cool down a room
37 Not old
38 "Ready, ___, go!"
40 Drink made by Lipton and Tetley

42 Popular brand of cookies: 2 words
48 "Little Miss Muffet sat ___ tuffet": 2 words
49 Someone who doesn't tell the truth
50 Be indebted to
51 Didn't lose
52 Aching
53 Country south of the United States: Abbreviation

DOWN

1 "___ your money where your mouth is!"
2 Gorilla
3 "___ and the Tramp"
4 "A little hard work never killed ___"
5 Keep telling someone to do something
6 It could become a swing that hangs from a branch
7 Someone who's forced to work for someone else
8 Sound from a sheep
9 Where the elbow is

10 "You bet!"

15 Scooby-___ (cartoon dog)

16 Lend a hand

19 Commercials

20 Last name of the author of "Curious George"

21 Sticky stuff that's used to make roads

23 One of Santa's helpers

25 Moving truck

26 Cubes in a freezer

27 Use a needle and thread

29 It can form on wet metal

31 Acting like an adult

34 Takes the skin off a fruit

36 It can be used to catch fish

39 Group of three singers

41 Part of a molecule

42 At this very moment

43 Colorful card game

44 Light brown

45 Candy ___ (sweet treat)

46 Lamb's mother

47 Tyrannosaurus ___ (big dinosaur)

3

ACROSS

1 Animals that purr
5 Instrument that an angel might play
9 Its capital is Des Moines
10 Robert ___ (general in the Civil War): 2 words
11 Cloth used for dusting
14 Got bigger
15 Person who tells fibs
16 State on the West Coast: Abbreviation
17 Swallowed
18 Big jungle animals
19 What people call you
20 Ranks
22 Not a single person
24 Hairy animals from Asia
26 Not far
27 Get
29 Closes
32 "Now hear ___!" ("Listen up!")
33 "You ___ be joking!"
35 Small bite
36 It's inside a football
37 Little lady

38 "Out of the frying pan, ___ the fire"
39 Pea container
40 Not to mention
41 Thaw
42 Red vegetable
43 George Washington was the first one: Abbreviation

DOWN

1 "Close but no ___!"
2 Large artery that delivers blood from the heart
3 Sylvester the Cat chased him: 2 words
4 Tool that cuts wood
5 Give assistance to
6 Martian, for example
7 Why something happens
8 Pay-___-view (kind of TV show)
11 Wile E. Coyote chased him: 2 words
12 Military group

13 "Golly!"

18 "___ silly question ...": 2 words

19 He built the ark, in the Bible

21 Chows down

23 Opposite of worst

25 "Cute as a button," for one

27 State that's west of Pennsylvania

28 Person who works in a hospital

30 It's on the front cover of a book

31 Markings on a leopard

32 Kind of dancing

34 The opening in a piggy bank that you put the coins into

37 Talk a lot

38 Little devil

4

ACROSS

1 ___ Turner (famous singer)
5 Use a shovel
8 What a record will do if you leave it out in the sun
12 Dr. Frankenstein's assistant
13 "___ good turn deserves another"
14 "That makes sense to me now": 2 words
15 One of the 13 original U.S. colonies: 2 words
18 TV ___
19 Welcome ___ (something to wipe your feet on)
20 "So ___, so good"
23 Large crowd
25 Campers sleep in them
29 "What have ___ to lose?": 2 words
31 Go faster than walking
33 Truth or ___ (game)
34 Mechanical "person"
36 Be a chatterbox
38 Dog's foot
39 "Under the ___" (song in "The Little Mermaid")
41 "Rub-a-dub-dub, three men in a ___"

43 One of the 13 original U.S. colonies
50 It's a Great Lake
51 That woman
52 ___ code (part of a phone number)
53 They can catch butterflies
54 Keep an ___ on (watch)
55 Changed the color of

DOWN

1 Some cans are made from it
2 "Where do ___ from here?": 2 words
3 Neither this ___ that
4 Martial ___ (karate, judo, etc.)
5 Person who heals the sick
6 Once ___ while: 2 words
7 It could cause you to get sick
8 Began to droop, like a flower
9 "___ was going to St. Ives ...": 2 words
10 ___ and Stimpy (cartoon pals)
11 Small round vegetable

16 It's at the bottom of a pants leg or skirt

17 A single grain

20 Kind of tree

21 Long ___ (many years back)

22 Steal from

24 Insect

26 Sleep for a little while

27 "___ la la" (sounds in a song)

28 Do some needlework

30 Throws

32 The environment

35 Drink that's made from leaves

37 Some people ride to school on one

40 Something that hurts

42 Small round thing on a necklace, sometimes

43 Guys

44 "How ___ you doing?"

45 Get into a chair

46 Word you might shout to get someone's attention

47 "___ it, you'll like it!"

48 Peg that a golf ball rests on

49 Unhappy

5

ACROSS

1 Slowly ___ surely
4 Weep
7 Meat eaten at breakfast
12 Put to good ___ (take advantage of)
13 Gardener's tool
14 Love a lot
15 Footwear worn at the beach
17 Made cuts in wood
18 Three times three
19 Tree branch
20 Artists use it
22 Fuel for a car
23 It's used to stop a squeaking sound
26 As well
27 "___ Arnold!" (Nickelodeon cartoon)
28 "Dr. Jekyll and Mr. ___"
29 "Fuzzy Wuzzy ___ a bear"
30 Grain that might come before "meal"
31 It's similar to an android
32 Joints near the middle of the body
34 Water ___ (sport played in a swimming pool)
35 Big guy in Archie Comics
37 Pastures
40 ___ a million: 2 words
41 "___ not my problem"
42 Kermit ___ Frog
43 Wooden poles on ships
44 "I have my heart ___ on it"
45 Female pig

DOWN

1 It takes kids to school
2 ___ Today (popular newspaper)
3 Andre Agassi wears them on his feet: 2 words
4 Say a witch's spell
5 Part played by an actor
6 Positive answer
7 On a first-name ___ with
8 The first man in the Bible
9 Garth Brooks wears them on his feet: 2 words
10 State north of California: Abbreviation
11 Homer's neighbor on "The Simpsons"

16 Fred Flintstone's pet

19 "Now I ___ me down to sleep ..."

20 Cat's hand

21 Apple pie ___ mode: 2 words

22 "I don't ___ it" ("Huh?")

24 Words at a wedding: 2 words

25 Allow

27 "Every cloud ___ a silver lining"

28 Grip

30 Unlocks

31 ___ beef (kind of meat)

33 "What time ___?": 2 words

34 ___ Rose (ballplayer who was banned from baseball)

35 Mother

36 "Humpty Dumpty sat ___ wall": 2 words

37 Prefix for "behave" or "spell"

38 "___ do you think you are?"

39 Make stitches

6

ACROSS

1 Get ___ of (remove)
4 Opposite of good
7 Insect that stings
10 Flying saucers: Abbreviation
12 You see with it
13 Part of an airplane
14 Kids can ride around on it: 2 words
16 Brand of frozen waffles
17 How to stop being hungry
18 ___ and crafts
20 What bran has that's good for you
23 ___ little while (soon): 2 words
24 Word that gets someone's attention
27 "___ was saying ...": 2 words
28 You might eat it with eggs
30 Need to repay
31 Old piece of material
32 Metal, when it's just been dug up
33 Goes out with
35 Fit ___ king (very nice): 2 words
37 Computer service with Buddy Lists and Instant Messages: Abbreviation
38 Put into storage
40 Someone who talks too much
45 It gets wrinkles out of clothes
46 Suffix for the word "hero"
47 It can be found in an orchard
48 Bottomless ___ (neverending hole)
49 "Jack ___ the Beanstalk"
50 Where someone would put a hearing aid

DOWN

1 ___ the wrong way (irritate)
2 "___ Ran the Circus" (Dr. Seuss book): 2 words
3 Hound
4 Red as a ___
5 How sailors say "yes"
6 Franklin ___ Roosevelt (former U.S. president)
7 Important person: 2 words
8 London's country: Abbreviation
9 A vain person has a big one

11 ___' Pea (Popeye's kid)

13 Drenched

15 Where ships come and go

19 At ___ (without any order or planning)

20 Distant

21 "This ___ job for Superman!": 2 words

22 Legendary hairy beast

23 ___ cream sundae

25 She's covered in wool

26 "That's right!"

29 Saudi ___ (country in the Middle East)

34 Plenty: 2 words

36 "Pick on somebody your ___ size!"

37 Turned another year older

38 Use a straw

39 Prefix for "cycle" or "angle"

41 Holiday ___ (chain of hotels)

42 Ending for "press" or "cult"

43 Drink that contains caffeine

44 ___ Majesty (how people refer to a queen)

7

ACROSS

1 He lived in the Garden of Eden

5 "As I was going to St. Ives, I met ___ with seven wives": 2 words

9 As easy as falling ___ a log

12 Coca-___

13 Challenge

14 "Prince ___" (song in the movie "Aladdin")

15 Blow a horn

16 You can go down a snowy hill on them

17 Pressed the doorbell

19 Remote control button that turns off the sound on the TV

21 Suffix that means "most"

22 Delayed

24 Hints

26 ___-back (easygoing)

27 What dry lips might do

28 You plant them in a garden

30 Bird that says "cock-a-doodle-doo!"

33 Where Dallas is: Abbreviation

34 What you carry food on, in a cafeteria

36 Person who battles the villain

37 Someone who lives in the Middle East

39 Sick as ___: 2 words

41 Taste a drink

42 Entertainer who makes gestures but doesn't talk

43 Destiny

44 Wooden peg used in golf

45 Irritating person

46 Barking up the wrong ___ (on the wrong track)

DOWN

1 Perform

2 "I'm ___!" ("I'll never make it!")

3 Read ___ (say the words on a page)

4 ___ Groening (creator of "The Simpsons")

5 They interrupt TV shows

6 A kid might take it after being sick during a quiz: 2 words

7 Get out of bed
8 Birds live in them
9 Paddles
10 Not bumpy
11 Kids take them at the end of the semester: 2 words
18 Happy
20 Sound in a canyon
23 Top-10 ___
25 Small hair above the eye
27 Road Runner chaser

28 It goes in the corner of an envelope
29 Spooky
30 Device that police use to catch speeders
31 One of the five Great Lakes
32 What you need to play tug-of-war
35 You can lay on one in the swimming pool
38 Gamble
40 "___ whiz!"

8

ACROSS

1 Criminals break them
5 Evenings: Abbreviation
8 Straight ___ arrow: 2 words
12 "I cannot tell ___": 2 words
13 Have dinner
14 "What ___ we thinking?"
15 Game players roll them
16 "How ___ supposed to know?": 2 words
17 "And they lived happily ___ after"
18 Big, hairy mountain animal
19 Word that can go after "space" or "witch"
21 Dead-___ street
22 Opposite of buys
24 Not the back
26 Female deer
27 "Pinky ___ the Brain"
28 Stoop down
30 What tourists like to have from their hotel windows
32 Letters after R
33 Bird with a red breast
35 King Kong, for one

37 Something that rhymes
39 ___ up (make into a small ball)
40 Tow
41 Location
42 Ending for "Japan"
43 The point ___ return: 2 words
44 What a broken bone has to do
45 Sign of the zodiac whose symbol is a lion
46 Forms a question

DOWN

1 Tramp's love, in a Disney movie
2 Fake name used by a criminal
3 She hated Snow White: 2 words
4 "___ you later, alligator!"
5 Certain fruits
6 One of the Three Bears
7 Hard, like a board
8 In ___ of (impressed by)
9 Snow White's friends: 2 words

10 "Well, ___ you sweet!"

11 Unpopular kid

19 "I read you loud and ___"

20 Locomotive

23 "Skip to My ___" (kids' song)

25 Kill two birds with ___ stone

28 Where to buy things

29 You use it after a shower

30 What the V stands for in VCR

31 Hit on the bottom

32 E-mail that you don't want

34 Second ___ (place in the infield)

36 Conceited people have big ones

38 Magazine that features "Spy Vs. Spy"

40 "___ good turn daily" (Boy Scout slogan): 2 words

9

ACROSS

1 What horses eat
5 Ending for "lion" or "host"
8 Cat that chased Jerry
11 "Where there's smoke, there's ___"
12 Parking ___ (place for cars)
13 You hear with it
14 You might roast them when camping
17 Jekyll turned into him
18 Typical score on a golf course
19 "You ___ My Sunshine"
21 Do some stitching
23 The capital of France
27 Jacket
29 ___ up (make more lively)
31 Coin from Mexico
32 ___ Murphy (actor in "Daddy Day Care")
34 Friend of Sleepy and Sneezy
36 Catch, as a criminal
37 Elementary school group: Abbreviation
39 Misplace
41 You might roast them when camping
46 Country south of Canada: Abbreviation
47 Big bird from Australia
48 Black-and-white cookie
49 24 hours
50 Piece of wood in a woodpile
51 Cincinnati ___ (baseball team)

DOWN

1 "Knock it ___!"
2 Dumb person
3 What breakfast in bed is served on
4 Puts in the mail
5 Toymaker at the North Pole
6 Chicken noodle ___
7 It holds a purse around a woman's shoulder
8 What a golf ball sits on
9 Canoe need
10 ___ Potato Head (toy)
15 "___ in touch!"

16 It might catch a mouse

19 Good card to have in blackjack

20 ___ and reel (fisherman's needs)

22 Marry

24 Got more issues of a magazine

25 "Patience ___ virtue": 2 words

26 Cry loudly

28 Amounts left for the waiters

30 Survey

33 Lucy's friend on "I Love Lucy"

35 Red, white, or blue

38 Short word for what goes into weapons

40 ___ loser (someone who hates not to win)

41 Wet dirt

42 Nutty ___ fruitcake: 2 words

43 Beam of sunshine

44 It follows July: Abbreviation

45 "Help me!"

ACROSS

1 Exercise that helps your stomach muscles: Hyphenated
6 Larger relative of a monkey
9 Tight ___ drum: 2 words
12 Big city in Nebraska
13 "In ___ We Trust" (phrase on U.S. money)
14 ___ Angeles (city in California)
15 Little red toy with wheels
16 School subject
18 "Mary ___ a little lamb"
20 "Holy cow!"
21 "What ___ supposed to do?": 2 words
24 "Give ___ break!": 2 words
26 Ready, willing, and ___
30 School subject: 2 words
34 Door openers
35 Ramada ___ (chain of hotels)
36 Spinning toy
37 The New York Knicks' group: Abbreviation
40 Tiny ___ (character in "A Christmas Carol")
42 School subject

46 Discusses
50 New Year's ___ (December 31)
51 The Mad Hatter drank it
52 Messages you get on the computer: Hyphenated
53 Not ___ (not so far)
54 Red meat
55 Father

DOWN

1 Female hog
2 "___ little teapot ...": 2 words
3 Game where you try not to be touched
4 "That's a problem": Hyphenated
5 Country that has a famous canal
6 How old you are
7 Ping-___
8 Cutting part of a knife
9 Muhammad ___ (famous boxer)
10 Desperate cry for help
11 Stuff at the bottom of a fireplace
17 Heavy metal

19 Its capital is Dover: Abbreviation

21 "Don't ___ me!" ("I have no idea")

22 One of the Three Stooges

23 Frosty

25 "Do ___ say!": 2 words

27 Little ___ (small amount)

28 One of the signs of the zodiac

29 Mind-reading ability, for short

31 "Money ___ everything"

32 Explosive stuff: Abbreviation

33 ___ States of America

38 This one and that one

39 Region

41 One of the Berenstain Bears

42 Homophone of "hay"

43 "___ got something to tell you"

44 All ___ (ready to go)

45 Thanksgiving vegetable

47 Boy

48 Baby goat

49 Sneaky

11

ACROSS

1 Leaves out
6 Little white lie
9 "That's ___, folks!"
12 Simple kind of boat
13 State that's south of Washington: Abbreviation
14 Cow's sound
15 Circus performer: 2 words
18 Travel on snow, in a way
19 "You can't teach an old dog ___ tricks"
20 ___-O-Honey (brand of candy)
23 Secret agent
25 Measured how long it took something to happen
29 Bad smell
31 Tool that has teeth
33 Jack or Jill, for example
34 Things with strings that go up and down: Hyphenated
36 Girl in "Little Women"
38 Kind of joke
39 Go ___ vacation: 2 words
41 Noah built one in the Bible
43 Circus performer: 2 words
50 Friend of Bashful and Grumpy
51 "This ___ stick-up!": 2 words
52 Appliance in the kitchen
53 Use a towel
54 Piece of wood in the fireplace
55 Made clothing

DOWN

1 Halloween's month: Abbreviation
2 Saint Patrick's Day's month: Abbreviation
3 ___ trance (hypnotized): 2 words
4 Toys that go around and around
5 Looks for
6 Enemy
7 Country that borders Iraq
8 French hat
9 "Where ___?" (question from a lost person): 2 words
10 ___ Angeles
11 "I have a ___ on my mind"
16 Closes up a sleeping bag

17 Identical ___ (lookalike relative)
20 Young man
21 "What can ___ to help?": 2 words
22 Plaything
24 Vegetable sometimes called a sweet potato
26 You might use one in a treasure hunt
27 Flightless bird from Australia
28 Where a lion lives
30 Kitchen or attic, for example

32 ___ and tear (day-to-day damage)
35 Very slow animal
37 Stuff in an Easter basket
40 Too
42 Windy day plaything
43 Do some arithmetic
44 Neither here ___ there
45 Covered in frozen water
46 Game where you try not to be It
47 ___ and then (occasionally)
48 Wife of Adam
49 Strawberry's color

ACROSS

1 Noah's ___
4 Word after "welcome" or "place"
7 Big party
11 Sound that a pigeon makes
12 "Roses ___ red ..."
13 Ending for "disk" or "major"
14 Eight: 3 words
17 Woman
18 "The piper's son," in a nursery rhyme
19 "... and a partridge in a ___ tree"
21 Normal score on a golf course
22 ___ and flow (what the tide does)
25 "Just ___ thought!": 2 words
26 "___ the rod and spoil the child"
28 Dessert that has a crust
29 It comes before Thursday: Abbreviation
30 "___ men are created equal"
31 Stop or Yield, for example
32 Go ___ diet: 2 words
33 Full-time athletes
35 Eight: 3 words
40 Gets older
41 Fishing pole
42 ___ good deed: 2 words
43 "What you don't know ___ hurt you"
44 Female animal on a farm
45 It's more than -er

DOWN

1 Put on an ___ (pretend)
2 Move a canoe
3 Fruity drink brand: Hyphenated
4 Woman who cleans a house
5 Part of the military
6 A golfer puts a ball on one
7 "Don't count your chickens ___ they hatch"
8 Tiny particle
9 Letters before V

10 Not him
15 Sticky black substance
16 "Twinkle Twinkle Little ___"
19 Puppy's hand
20 Ending for "Siam"
21 Good friend
22 Chapter
23 Large
24 ___ Affleck (famous actor)
26 Least crazy
27 Plot

31 Letters that signal for help
32 Microwave ___
33 Farming tool that breaks up the soil
34 Impolite
35 Looked at
36 A conceited person has a big one
37 It can come before "school" or "teen"
38 Negative answers
39 Dine

ACROSS

1 Italian food
6 The past tense of "is"
9 Typical
10 "Prince ___" (song in "Aladdin")
11 Simple bed for a camper
14 Young lion in "The Lion King"
15 Tiny ___ (character in "A Christmas Carol")
16 Boat rower
17 Meat from a pig
18 Horn's sound
19 America, for short
20 ___ Fudd (cartoon character)
23 Hedgehog in video games
25 ___ out (cover a wide area)
27 Fluffy chocolate dessert
28 Crunchy Mexican foods
29 Stressed out
30 One thing ___ time (not all together): 2 words
31 ___ on the cob
33 Place to put a napkin
36 The edge of a drinking glass
37 Chopping tool
38 Stringed instrument
40 At the ___ of one's lungs (very loudly)
41 ___ and Stimpy (cartoon pair)
42 An archer shoots one
43 Now ___ then
44 Birds build them

DOWN

1 Opposite of pull
2 Very large continent
3 Where some kids go in June: 2 words
4 It fits into a slot
5 State next to Mississippi: Abbreviation
6 Word that goes before "melon" or "logged"
7 "I cannot tell ___": 2 words
8 Last name of Homer and Marge
11 People who work at 3-Down

12 Place in the desert that's not so bad

13 Copy a drawing

18 Sleeping place

21 A sign of the zodiac

22 Makeup for eyelashes

24 Ending for "danger"

25 Beginning

26 Area of a house where there might be a barbecue

27 Guys

29 Something that's very popular for the time being

32 Big animals that look like yaks

34 Very much: 2 words

35 Dogs walk on them

38 Movers' truck

39 Dublin's country: Abbreviation

14

ACROSS

1 ___ gun (toy weapon)
4 School subject
8 Animal represented by Capricorn in the zodiac
12 Grease
13 Tell ___ (be dishonest): 2 words
14 Ending for "respect"
15 "___ makes perfect"
17 "Peekaboo, ___ you!": 2 words
18 Answers that are negative
19 Thirteen minus twelve
20 Way to lose weight
22 Ace or king, for example
25 It surrounds a basketball net
28 Columbus Day's month: Abbreviation
29 Fought with fists
30 It's used to record TV shows: Abbreviation
31 Boston ___ Party
32 Was in debt to
33 There are seven of these in a week
34 Take money from
36 Sizzling
37 It's east of Europe
39 Yellow fruits
44 Sulk
45 Enjoy a magazine
46 Kanga's kid in "Winnie-the-Pooh"
47 Certain trees
48 Cassette
49 What a nod means

DOWN

1 Police officer
2 Your lungs need it
3 Place to see stars and moons
4 Things in front of doors that say "Welcome"
5 Muhammad ___
6 ___ Tacs (brand of breath mints)
7 "Tee-___!" (giggle)
8 ___ weight (get heavy)
9 Place to see stars and moons
10 Ginger ___
11 Wooden item used by golfers
16 You might put a sleeping bag on it

19 Unusual
20 Part of a lowercase letter "I"
21 ___ cream sandwich
22 Animal that has udders
23 Tool that cuts down trees
24 ___ rover (playground game)
26 Covered in frost
27 ___ Paul's (brand of fish sticks)
29 ___ for apples

33 One of the Seven Dwarfs
35 Grains that horses eat
36 ___ and seek
37 Relative of a baboon
38 Note before la
39 Stuff in museums
40 "The Princess and the ___"
41 P. Diddy's music
42 Body part that has a nail
43 Letters used during an emergency

15

ACROSS

1 Remain
5 ___ squad (group of cheerleaders)
8 Toys that spin around
12 "That's not good!": 2 words
13 ___ of corn
14 Solemn vow
15 Where the throat is
16 Fish that can cause a person pain
18 Spider-Man, for one
20 The Caspian ___ (body of water)
21 Bullwinkle was one
23 ___ good deed (be helpful): 2 words
24 "Don't ___ all your eggs into one basket"
27 Letters after S
28 Secret ___ (spy)
30 "... and pretty maids all ___ row": 2 words
31 It contains pigs
32 Young woman, in slang
33 Mistake
35 Soup container
36 ___ code (part of a phone number)
37 Fish that's frequently eaten
41 Cost an arm ___ leg: 2 words
44 Incorrect way to say "aren't"
45 Ending for "differ"
46 Pork ___
47 Pegs on golf courses
48 Drivers drive on them: Abbreviation
49 Really dislike

DOWN

1 Male child
2 Start of many book titles
3 Fish that is on some pizzas
4 They're used to join up oxen
5 Coin in Mexico
6 Have some food
7 Jail
8 An old Roman would wear one
9 Boat paddle
10 Elementary school group: Abbreviation
11 Not outgoing

17 More organized
19 The president after Carter
21 The Rockies, for example: Abbreviation
22 "For crying ___ loud!"
23 State next to Maryland: Abbreviation
24 Fish that has very sharp teeth
25 Game with "Skip" cards
26 "Br'er Rabbit and the ___ Baby"
29 Goose's husband
34 Get to
35 Uses scissors
36 ___ and crafts
37 Overweight
38 "Let sleeping dogs ___"
39 Number of wheels on a unicycle
40 "I'm at the ___ of my rope!"
42 Period
43 Strong jungle animal

16

ACROSS

1 Tramp
5 Young deer
9 ___ on the back (encouragement)
12 "... I met ___ with seven wives": 2 words
13 A Great Lake
14 Word yelled to encourage a bullfighter
15 Guys' dates
16 New York baseball team
17 One-sixtieth of an hour: Abbreviation
18 "I knew it!"
19 Rip ___ Winkle
20 Makes less wild
22 Was in a footrace
23 Applaud
25 Boy's name that sounds the same as the girl's name "Jean"
26 Make well
28 Rod and ___ (fishing equipment)
30 "___ the cat's away, the mice will play"
32 Twirl around
34 ___ on rye (kind of sandwich)

37 Something you do all the time
39 Bread ___ butter
40 State south of Washington: Abbreviation
41 Tennessee ___ (space in Monopoly): Abbreviation
42 Direction where the sun rises
44 Spoiled kid
45 Drink that's popular in England
46 Ending for "disk"
47 Where Russia is
48 Uncle ___ (symbol of America)
49 Opposite of "far"
50 Show and ___

DOWN

1 "___ the Horrible" (comic strip)
2 Large city in Nebraska
3 Gymnastics event: 2 words
4 Slip-___ (shoes you don't need to tie)
5 Women
6 Sports stadium

7 Sense of humor
8 Home in a tree
9 Gymnastics event: 2 words
10 Marvin the Martian, for example
11 Past ___ (like the verb "was")
19 It connects to a TV: Abbreviation
21 Number of years you've been alive
24 It connects to a computer

27 Prefix with "corn" or "cycle"
29 From beginning to ___
30 "___ up, doc?"
31 "___ nice day!": 2 words
33 Spaghetti or macaroni, for example
35 Thin as ___: 2 words
36 Aluminum, for one
38 Someone who's not 20 yet
43 Had a snack
44 It hits a baseball

17

ACROSS

1 Homer Simpson's cry
4 Walk in shallow water
8 Throw
12 "Are there ___ questions?"
13 Take down ___ (make someone humble): 2 words
14 ___ instant (very quickly): 2 words
15 Highway: Abbreviation
16 Popular Italian food
18 Very heavy weights
20 "... or ___!" (end of a threat)
21 Part of the body near the middle
22 Black-and-white Chinese animals
24 Word at the end of a hymn
26 Bird that eats mice
27 Make an effort
28 Film about a pig that wants to be a sheepdog
30 Squanders
33 You might put it in a frame
34 Like a villain

36 Magicians pull rabbits out of them
38 They're often served on top of 16-Across
41 Sticky stuff used to make syrup
42 Man
43 Captain Hook's assistant
44 A self-centered person has a big one
45 State that's north of Texas: Abbreviation
46 Small pie
47 "___ me make this perfectly clear ..."

DOWN

1 It can be thrown at a bull's-eye
2 "___ of old Smokey ...": 2 words
3 Laughing ___ (kind of animal)
4 Used to be
5 Have a second trial
6 Hands out cards
7 Food that is sold by the dozen

8 Make a knot
9 Corn ___ cob: 2 words
10 Smooth fabric
11 Small cut
17 Listens
19 Someone who looks down on other people
23 Nerdy person
25 Story about Greek gods
27 More like a skyscraper
28 Snap in two

29 Not ___ (not even slightly): 2 words
30 Fred Flintstone's wife
31 It props up a painting
32 Where a play takes place
33 Bullets, for short
35 Very wide
37 "X marks the ___"
39 The mad ___ party (scene in "Alice in Wonderland")
40 "On your mark, get ___, go!"

18

ACROSS

1 Superman wears one
5 It's between the shoulder and the wrist
8 Abbreviation at the end of a list
11 Where Vietnam is
12 What oobleck is, in Dr. Seuss's "Bartholomew and the Oobleck"
13 Cindy-___ Who (girl in "How the Grinch Stole Christmas!")
14 Start of a nursery rhyme: 2 words, 1 hyphenated
17 ___-Hoo (brand of chocolate drink)
18 ___ as a bug in a rug
19 Not bright
22 Country that became independent in 1776: Abbreviation
24 Line you make in your hair
27 Prefix that means "one"
28 Its capital is Austin
31 At this very moment
32 Crunchy vegetable
34 Ending for the word "insist"
35 "If it's not ___ much trouble ..."

36 Someone who lives in the Middle East
39 "One ___ customer": 2 words
41 Start of a nursery rhyme: 3 words
46 "___ work and no play makes Jack a dull boy"
47 Summertime zodiac sign
48 Black-eyed ___
49 ___ Willie Winkie
50 Conclusion
51 When Labor Day is: Abbreviation

DOWN

1 Sacramento's state: Abbreviation
2 "Just ___ suspected!": 2 words
3 Feel sorry for
4 Go to a restaurant: 2 words
5 Ice ___ (very cold period in Earth's history)
6 Is a thief
7 People first landed on it in 1969
8 Very stylish
9 Part of the foot
10 Half a pint

15 Misplace

16 Young dog

19 The Dynamic ___ (Batman and Robin)

20 Writing fluid

21 Something that can't be explained

23 Wood-chopping tool

25 Character in "Winnie-the-Pooh"

26 "___ heads are better than one"

29 Prefix that means "against"

30 Walks loudly

33 Noah built one in Genesis

37 Ending for "port" or "depend"

38 "I've ___ working on the railroad ..."

40 Busy as ___: 2 words

41 Bone at the bottom of the face

42 Ginger ___ (type of soft drink)

43 Show agreement

44 ___ up (drink like a dog)

45 It means "most" when it's at the end of a word

19

ACROSS

1 People step on them when they get out of the shower
5 Girl pigs
9 It has 50 states: Abbreviation
12 "What's ___ for me?": 2 words
13 "What a relief!"
14 Box that contains the parts for a model car
15 Musical instrument that you hit with small hammers
17 "___ only as directed" (instruction on medicine)
18 Lemon meringue ___
19 "___ me about it!"
21 It's used to make maple syrup
24 Give it a shot
26 ___-weeny
29 "That's just the way ___": 2 words
31 It might be pierced
33 Paste
34 Was in a fast competition
36 "___ Goes the Weasel"
38 Ending for "absorb"
39 "I couldn't ___ less!"
41 "Who Wants to ___ Millionaire": 2 words

43 Expert
45 Musical instrument that you squeeze
50 Kind of fuel
51 "___ do you want?"
52 Measure of land
53 A conceited person has a big one
54 Father's boys
55 "Pleased to ___ you!"

DOWN

1 Stir up
2 "Baa baa black sheep, have you ___ wool?"
3 "Open 9 ___ 5" (sign on a store window)
4 What a red light means
5 Shape of a ball
6 Exclamation similar to "Aha!"
7 ___ away (disappeared)
8 Tasting like sugar
9 Musical instrument that you strum
10 Brother's sibling, for short
11 Homophone of "eight"
16 The stone in the middle of a peach

20 Chicken drumstick
21 What a private calls a sergeant, in the army
22 ___ moment's notice (with no warning): 2 words
23 Musical instrument that you blow into
25 Shrill bark from a dog
27 Woman who wears an outfit called a habit
28 "Are we there ___?"
30 The Mediterranean ___ (body of water)
32 Mechanical creatures

35 Makes a picture
37 Revolutions ___ minute (what RPM stands for)
40 Sound in a cave
42 ___ and Eve
43 Edgar Allan ___ (famous American writer)
44 Big ___ (nickname for a large truck)
46 "You ___ do it!"
47 Skate on thin ___ (do something risky)
48 Raw metal
49 A trapeze artist might fall into it

20

ACROSS

1 Small baked dessert
5 "How long ___ this been going on?"
8 Rock back and forth
12 Where Korea is
13 Get ready to shoot a basketball
14 White-faced
15 Group for some young people: 3 words
18 You hear with it
19 Spike ___ (famous movie director)
20 Help someone get higher
23 Places to store clothes
27 "Mind your ___ business!"
28 Mother's Day is in this month
29 The note after fa
30 You can make a milkshake in one
33 Not full
35 Long, slippery fish
36 "Who am ___ say?": 2 words
37 Group for some young people: 2 words
44 Had a debt
45 Home of a lion
46 What "expectorate" is a fancy word for
47 Marries
48 Not ___ (not so far)
49 Simple

DOWN

1 Tic-___-toe
2 Clean ___ whistle: 2 words
3 The outer part of a basketball hoop
4 Records on a VCR
5 A barber cuts it
6 Vanish into thin ___
7 Stinky
8 Secret agents
9 The Revolutionary ___
10 ___ thumbs (clumsy)
11 "That's true"
16 Not thin
17 Prefix that means "earth"
20 "___ the Builder" (kids' show)
21 Bird that's awake at night
22 Low number
23 Station wagon, for example

24 The "sixth sense": Abbreviation
25 Baby
26 ___ as a fox
28 The music in a song
31 Has to have
32 The first state to sign the Constitution: Abbreviation
33 "And so forth": Abbreviation
34 Large animal from Canada

36 "Money ___ everything!"
37 "That's really impressive!"
38 Female animal that has wool
39 Place for napping
40 Use your eyes
41 Open ___ can of worms: 2 words
42 "___ the season to be jolly ..."
43 Where a pig might live

21

ACROSS

1 Traffic ___ (driving problems)
5 "Now I know my ___ ..." (line in the alphabet song)
9 ___ Moines (city in Iowa)
12 Woodwind instrument
13 Small pie
14 Ending for "devil" or "child"
15 Small piece of land in the sea
16 Where India is
17 You eat soup with it
19 Light ___ feather: 2 words
21 Door unlocker
22 ___-it-all (smart aleck)
23 Dull color
24 Ending for "host"
25 What the T stands for in "TV"
27 Direction on a compass
29 "___, humbug!" (what Scrooge said)
31 Insects that live in hills
33 "Yeah, sure!": 2 words
36 Prefix that means "the environment"
37 Pay-___-view (kind of TV show)
38 Video-game company
39 Old-style word for "you"
41 It's inside an hourglass
43 Jar covering
44 "I made a mistake"
45 ___ tea (cool drink)
46 Robert E. ___ (famous military leader)
47 Mr. Potato Head piece
48 Collections

DOWN

1 Put together
2 Stomach muscles, for short
3 Kind of tooth
4 Teeter-totters
5 One step ___ time: 2 words
6 Certain sport
7 Weeps
8 Remains
9 Floppy ___ (thing that goes into a computer)
10 Cable channel that shows sports: Abbreviation

11 Play 6-Down: 2 words
18 Homophone for “oh”
20 How sailors say “yes”
23 The first book of the Bible
26 It disappears when you stand up
28 Settle into a chair
29 “Don’t ___ it!” (“I doubt it!”): 2 words
30 Sound of a sneeze
32 Make a silhouette
34 Lake that borders Pennsylvania
35 High ___ (when waves come closest to the shore)
38 Puts numbers together
40 “What’s the ___ of trying?” (quitter’s question)
42 You need one to play volleyball

22

ACROSS

1 Snow day vehicle
5 When the sun comes up
9 Scientist's room
12 Homophone of "pail"
13 Where Toledo is
14 "May ___ excused?": 2 words
15 High cards in many games
16 Lays out in the sun
17 Stuff that makes hair stiffer
18 Packs of cards
20 Lucy's friend on "I Love Lucy"
22 Word ending that means "most"
23 Fat as ___: 2 words
27 ___-bitty
28 Makes fun of
31 Turn around
33 "Finding ___" (2003 Disney movie)
34 "It ___ no trouble at all"
37 Insects that sometimes live on dogs
39 The most common last name in America
41 "___ Baba and the Forty Thieves"

42 Girl on "The Simpsons"
46 Boy's name that reads the same forward and backward
47 Decay
48 Hot thing in the kitchen
49 Sound that comes back after you say it
50 Messy place
51 Plant that you don't want in a garden
52 "That woman is," as a contraction

DOWN

1 Black playing card, sometimes
2 Shoestrings
3 It's used to make a room bright
4 Where you sit in a classroom
5 Polka ___ (circle on a fabric)
6 "Now I understand!"
7 Come in first place
8 It smells
9 It's used to make a room bright: 2 words

10 Red as ___: 2 words
11 Stomach
19 Down in the dumps
21 Equal score for both teams
24 ___ the tail on the donkey
25 Put frosting on a cake
26 Bubble ___
29 It's inside a pen
30 ___ Angeles, California
31 ___ and stripes (things on a U.S. flag)

32 Plane flyer
35 ___ last minute (when procrastinators do things): 2 words
36 Tells to go away
38 Not fast
40 Tavern on "The Simpsons"
43 "___ had it up to here!"
44 Wait and ___ (don't rush into things)
45 Tom ___ Jerry (cartoon pair)

23

ACROSS

1 Something that's popular for a short time

4 What a baseball player wears on his head

7 Slowly ___ surely

10 Bunches: 2 words

12 "Rub-a-dub-dub, three men ___ tub": 2 words

13 Number that appears on a penny

14 President from 1969 to 1974: 2 words

17 "And so on": Abbreviation

18 First woman in the Bible

19 Kind of music

22 Worker for Santa

24 Misplay in a baseball game

28 Decorated cupcakes

30 Part of the head

32 ___ and sound

33 ___ badge (what a Boy Scout earns)

35 A golf ball rests on top of it

37 Magazine with the catchphrase "What, me worry?"

38 Word before "shore" or "shell"

40 Place to work out

42 President from 1981 to 1989: 2 words

48 "So ___ me!" (sarcastic remark)

49 Don't tell the truth

50 Toy that goes up and down: Hyphenated

51 Attempt

52 ___ a good example

53 Mountain ___ (brand of soft drink)

DOWN

1 "So ___, so good"

2 Aladdin pretended to be this prince, in the movie

3 "What's up, ___?"

4 Round shape

5 "Cross my heart ___ hope to die"

6 Part of a window

7 Professional fighters

8 Colorful card game

9 Five times two

11 "King of ___ Hill" (TV cartoon)

15 Gobbled up

16 "___ got an idea!"

19 Outer edge
20 Valuable card in many games
21 Miles ___ gallon (what MPG stands for)
23 "___ Albert" (old cartoon show)
25 Male sheep
26 "Birds ___ feather flock together": 2 words
27 One of the primary colors
29 Movie company that made "The Lion King"
31 Feel sorry about
34 Popular drink in England
36 Private ___ (detective)
39 "___ well that ends well"
41 Mother ___ I (game)
42 Letters between Q and U
43 Your and my
44 Opposite of "live"
45 "In ___ we trust" (U.S. motto)
46 Yes, in the military
47 Not later

24

ACROSS

1 A ___ off the old block
5 Animal that oinks
8 Yosemite ___ (cartoon character)
11 "What are you talking ___?"
13 Friend of Tigger and Eeyore
14 Country in North America: Abbreviation
15 Football score
17 Catch forty winks
18 Door opener
19 Middle-___ (neither young nor old)
21 Brother's relative, for short
24 Word that starts four state names
26 Make noises while sleeping
29 Fix mistakes in writing
31 Beavers might build one in a river
33 Identical ___ (lookalike relative)
34 Carried
36 "Where ___ go from here?": 2 words
38 ___ off (start to fall asleep)
39 Bambi was one
41 ___ distance (far away): 2 words

43 Long ___ (not recently)
45 Numbers said in reverse order before a rocket launch
50 ___ and then (occasionally)
51 They try to sell things
52 Enthusiastic cry from a cowboy
53 Very heavy weight
54 What the French word "oui" means in English
55 Cuts the grass

DOWN

1 Lion or leopard, for example
2 Cable channel that shows lots of movies: Abbreviation
3 It shows that you're in debt to someone
4 What a hockey player hits
5 ___ and con (sides in a debate)
6 State in the Midwest
7 Instruments that make deep sounds when you hit them
8 The beginning of the evening
9 White ___ ghost: 2 words

10 Cartographer's creation
12 Now and ___
16 Changed something's color, in a way
20 Suffix for "differ"
21 ___ sail (leave in a boat)
22 Phrase during a wedding: 2 words
23 Stop standing: 2 words
25 ___ up (crumple, as a piece of paper)
27 ___ de Janeiro (city in Brazil)
28 Dead-___ street
30 Peg used by Tiger Woods
32 ___ and groan
35 Go bad

37 ___-bitty (small)
40 Was a passenger in a car
42 Eve's husband
43 Small insect
44 What gak was, on the game show "Double Dare"
46 The ___ Enterprise ("Star Trek" spacecraft)
47 Exclamation that reads the same forward and backward
48 Exclamation that reads the same forward and backward
49 1, 2, and 3, for example: Abbreviation

25

ACROSS

1 It might be in a garage
4 "What ___ know?":
2 words
7 The Red ___ (Snoopy's enemy)
12 Number that changes on your birthday
13 Homophone of "or"
14 Be ___ of (know about)
15 Bottom's opposite
16 Enjoy a winter sport
17 "A Boy ___ Charlie Brown"
18 Tell a whopper
20 Command to a dog
22 "As I was going to St. Ives, I met ___ with seven wives": 2 words
24 "Better late ___ never"
25 Abbreviation before a wife's name
28 Breed of dog: 2 words
31 Female who says "baa"
32 What you pay to be in a club
33 Game of observation:
2 words
34 Try to lose weight
35 ___ and downs
36 "It's ___ time!" ("Finally!")

39 "___ the season to be jolly ..."
41 "___ no wonder!"
44 Daniel ___ (legendary frontiersman)
45 Mother of Cain and Abel
46 Zodiac sign that comes after Cancer
47 ___ with (dealt with)
48 Color of a cherry
49 Sea creature that's long and thin

DOWN

1 Siamese or Persian, for example
2 A while ___ (in the past)
3 Find a substitute for
4 Amount of medicine
5 Tree that has acorns
6 Breed of dog: 2 words
7 Yellow fruit
8 "___ in a Manger" (Christmas carol)
9 Male who says "baa"
10 What metal is called when it has just been mined

11 Mr. Flanders on "The Simpsons"
19 Liquid that people write with
21 Water faucets
22 Good card to have in blackjack
23 Cut the grass
24 Choice on some tests
25 Weapon that flies through the air
26 Democrat's opponent: Abbreviation
27 Sneaky
29 Fixed a newspaper article
30 Small bite
34 Hill of sand
35 Like cars that aren't new
36 Start of the alphabet
37 Kid in "Monsters, Inc."
38 Alley-___ (kind of shot in basketball)
40 "Now ___ seen everything!"
42 Little thing used in golf
43 Note between fa and ti

26

ACROSS

1 Sat for an artist
6 The last word in the Pledge of Allegiance
9 Part of a minute: Abbreviation
12 "On the ___ hand ..."
13 Zodiac sign that comes before Virgo
14 Sticky stuff used to make a road
15 Took illegally
16 ___ enforcement (police officers)
17 "Two heads ___ better than one"
18 Stitch
19 Drivers brake at them: 2 words
22 Ending for "north" or "south"
23 Piglet's mother
24 Bulletproof ___ (something a cop might wear)
25 How military people say "yes"
26 Go "boo-hoo"
28 "___ goes around, comes around"
31 "So ___ me!"
32 ___ Antonio, Texas
35 Drivers brake at them: 2 words
38 It comes with a cup of soda
39 Sam-___ (Dr. Seuss character): Hyphenated
40 ___ the knot (get married)
41 A car has four of them
43 Prefix that means "three"
44 New Year's ___
45 Important happening
46 At the end of a word, it means more than "-er"
47 "You've ___ your match!"
48 Bumps in cars' fenders

DOWN

1 Group of people in a Western movie
2 Playful river animal
3 Revealed
4 Electric ___ (fish that can shock you)
5 In a nice outfit
6 Permit
7 Jump

8 Highs and ___

9 Where the actors are, in a theater

10 Deserves

11 Brand of toothpaste

20 ___ shoes (things a ballerina wears)

21 Poison ___ (plant that can make you itch)

25 Ocean that borders Florida: Abbreviation

26 "___ it out!" ("Quit it!")

27 Took a quick break

28 Put words on paper

29 Uses one's ears

30 "___ one" (phrase on a ticket)

31 Bed covering

32 Noisy thing on top of a fire truck

33 Without ___ (penniless): 2 words

34 Robins' homes

36 Thing

37 Donate

42 "___ got an idea!"

27

ACROSS

1 What a happy dog's tail will do
4 "Curiosity killed the ___"
7 Three-piece ___
11 King Kong was one
12 Be untruthful
13 Me, myself, ___: 2 words
14 Where some poor students have to go: 2 words
17 Body of water
18 Burnt ___ crisp: 2 words
19 Bark from a chihuahua
22 Vincent Van Gogh made it
24 Take ___ in your work
28 Shake ___ (hurry): 2 words
30 Take a small drink of
32 China and Japan are there
33 Noisy instrument you hum into
35 Stay ___ (don't move)
37 Was introduced to
38 Insect that might go to a picnic
40 You can boil water in it
42 Skiing, skating, etc.: 2 words

48 "___ what you mean": 2 words
49 Card with an A in the corner
50 "I get it!"
51 Opening in a fence
52 ___ bull terrier (dog breed)
53 To this point

DOWN

1 "Who ___ that masked man?"
2 Manjula's husband on "The Simpsons"
3 Jewels
4 Wipes clean
5 Atmosphere
6 Examination
7 The largest desert in the world
8 One, in Spain
9 Bride and groom's words: 2 words
10 "Open 9 ___ 5" (sign on a store door)
15 "Give ___ break!": 2 words
16 Short word for a police officer

19 Big hairy animal from Tibet
20 State that borders Florida: Abbreviation
21 Candy that comes out of a dispenser
23 "It's on the ___ of my tongue"
25 Ending for "real" or "symbol"
26 What batteries eventually do
27 Enjoy food
29 Type of facial hair
31 Marionette, for example
34 Three minus two
36 ___ good to be true
39 It might catch a rat
41 What hospital food comes on
42 False hair
43 "This ___ stick-up!": 2 words
44 What a basketball goes through
45 ___-fi (kind of fiction)
46 On ___ double (quickly)
47 Was on a chair

28

ACROSS

1 "Charlotte's ___"
4 Network that airs "Survivor": Abbreviation
7 People form these when they sit down
11 "A long time ___, in a galaxy far, far away ..."
12 Ginger ___ (bubbly drink)
13 Try to shoot: 2 words
14 Slime
15 Short people in 26-Across
17 Joint in the leg
19 "___-haw" (what a donkey says)
20 Small piece of land surrounded by water
22 Iced ___ (cold drink)
23 ___ Baba
26 Movie starring Judy Garland: 4 words
30 Television ___
31 Tiny bite
32 Encourage
33 Cable channel that shows news 24 hours a day: Abbreviation
34 Response to the Little Red Hen: 2 words
36 Brainless character in 26-Across
40 You drink out of it

43 "Peter, Peter, pumpkin ___ ..."
44 Raggedy ___ (doll)
45 "___ matter of fact ...": 2 words
46 Part of a cat's paw
47 "That's right"
48 You can catch butterflies with it

DOWN

1 A dog's tail might do it
2 A modest person has a small one
3 Small publication
4 Arrived
5 Color on the American flag
6 Member of Congress: Abbreviation
7 Fit ___ a glove
8 "What a good boy ___!" (what Little Jack Horner said): 2 words
9 Frying ___
10 Roads and avenues: Abbreviation
13 ___ of schedule (early)
16 She sang the song "Believe"
18 ___ Mexico (U.S. state)

1	2	3		4	5	6			7	8	9	10
11				12				13				
14				15		16						
		17	18				19					
20	21					22				23	24	25
26				27	28			29				
30				31					32			
		33				34	35					
36	37	38			39				40	41	42	
43					44				45			
46					47				48			

20 "For what ___ worth ..."
21 This female
22 Noisy kind of dance
23 From Egypt or Kenya, perhaps
24 ___ cabin (wooden house)
25 Ending for "organ" or "alphabet"
27 ___ tube
28 One of the metals used to make brass
29 ___ of control
33 The people who work on a ship

34 ___ of the above (quiz choice)
35 Possesses
36 Fraction of a minute: Abbreviation
37 Where San Francisco is: Abbreviation
38 One ___ time: 2 words
39 Word that can come after "X" or "sting"
41 Put to good ___ (take advantage of)
42 ___ Sajak ("Wheel of Fortune" host)

29

ACROSS

1 Taxi
4 People travel down rivers on them
9 Health resort
12 100%
13 Have the same opinion
14 Joint near the middle of the body
15 ___ Grande (Texas river)
16 Not a single person: 2 words
17 "Hot," to "cold": Abbreviation
18 What people who live in apartments pay
20 Like numbers that aren't divisible by two
21 ___ race
23 It may be glazed or jelly-filled
26 Small earthquake
28 Trees that are used in making syrup
31 ___ Jackson (popular female singer)
33 Sound from a pig's nose
34 State that's west of Georgia: Abbreviation
36 "Darn it!"
38 Go ___ vacation: 2 words
39 Tooth ___ (what eating too much sugar can cause)
42 "Do ___ say!": 2 words
43 The center of a cherry
44 Joint near the foot
45 "Cross my heart and hope to ___"
46 Look at
47 He received the Ten Commandments in the Bible
48 ___, nose, and throat (specialty of some doctors)

DOWN

1 Suitcase that you can bring aboard a plane: Hyphenated
2 Tell ___ (be untruthful): 2 words
3 Having yellowish hair
4 Was in charge of
5 "Give it ___!" ("Try it!"): 2 words
6 Round cereal: 2 words
7 "I ___ to agree" ("I basically think so, too")
8 Item planted in a garden

9 Not tall

10 Pied ___ (character in a children's story)

11 Round cereal: 2 words

19 ___ Hanks (famous actor who was the voice of Woody in "Toy Story")

22 "I ___ bear of very little brain" (Winnie-the-Pooh quote): 2 words

24 More disgusting

25 Network that aired "Buffy the Vampire Slayer": Abbreviation

27 Stop sign's color

29 Bert's roommate on "Sesame Street"

30 South Carolina or South Dakota, for example

32 Swap

34 He lived in the Garden of Eden

35 Jay ___ (host of "The Tonight Show")

37 Where Afghanistan is

40 Ginger ___ (type of beverage)

41 Positive answer

30

ACROSS

1 The answer to an addition problem
4 Sticky stuff that comes out of a tree
7 Place for an infant
11 ___ little while (soon): 2 words
12 Dessert that has a crust
13 Not early
14 A kid might sit on it for fun: 2 words
17 You need one to play ping-pong
18 Make ___ of (find something to do with)
19 Men
22 Prefix that means "before"
23 "___ what I mean?"
26 Long, skinny musical instrument
27 Jack Sprat couldn't eat it
28 Large town
29 When Halloween is: Abbreviation
30 Hot, black, sticky stuff
31 Waltz or tango, for example
32 Dad's wife
33 Daughter's brother
34 A kid might sit on it for fun: Hyphenated
40 Weather ___ (thing on a roof)
41 People need it to live
42 "What do I ___ you?" ("How much money do I have to pay?")
43 Really surprise
44 ___ Butterworth's (brand of syrup)
45 Middle of the school week: Abbreviation

DOWN

1 ___ Lancelot (famous knight)
2 Game that includes "Draw 4" cards
3 Big ___ (kind of hamburger)
4 Undercover agents
5 "___ I a stinker?" (line from Bugs Bunny)
6 It's used to hold a tent in place
7 Shut
8 Uncommon
9 "___ a miracle!"
10 Insect that lives in a hive
15 "... with a banjo on my ___" (line in "Oh Susanna")

16 Feel pain
19 What cows say
20 Easy as ___
21 Parking ___ (place for many cars)
22 Normal score on a golf course
23 "It's a ___ to tell a lie"
24 "And on and on": Abbreviation
25 Where the pupil and cornea are
27 ___ and fortune (what celebrities have)
28 "I ___ believe it!"

30 "On a scale from one ___ ...": 2 words
31 You leave rooms through them
32 It shows what a restaurant serves
33 Mix together
34 Couch potatoes watch them: Abbreviation
35 Consume
36 Butt into
37 ___ truck (vehicle that picks up stranded cars)
38 She gives birth to a lamb
39 Bright color

31

ACROSS

1 Touch gently, as with a washcloth
4 Finds the total
8 Made of frilly white fabric
12 North American nation: Abbreviation
13 Material that comes from sheep
14 Shrek, for one
15 Football team from Texas: 2 words
18 Eat ___ a bird
19 ___ Willie Winkie
20 Glittered
22 Fast airplane
23 Stuck in a ___
26 You catch a fish on it
27 The Civil ___
28 The ___ Ranger
29 Money used in Japan
30 Walking on ___ (very happy)
31 Hot drink popular in the winter
32 "___ aboard!"
33 Bag
34 Football team from Florida: 2 words
40 Measure of farmland

41 One of the five Great Lakes
42 Fish that's hard to catch
43 Someone between 12 and 20 years old
44 Baseball team from Cincinnati
45 Place for pigs

DOWN

1 Firecracker that doesn't go off
2 High ___ kite: 2 words
3 Hot-air ___
4 Not asleep
5 How much medicine you're supposed to take
6 "Snow White and the Seven Dwarfs" person
7 Less speedy
8 Part of the ear where an earring goes
9 Long ___ (many years back)
10 What chopping onions might make you do
11 Opposite of "no"
16 Part of a chain

17 Covered in water
20 Afraid to meet new people
21 Tool used in the garden
22 Container for jelly
23 Mountain range in the western United States
24 Numero ___ (#1)
25 "It's not my cup of ___"
27 Not as tame
28 The ___ Ness Monster (Scottish beast)
30 Muhammad ___ (famous fighter)

31 Some superheroes wear them
32 Word at the end of a prayer
33 Moved on a slippery surface
34 Welcome ___ (something to wipe your feet on)
35 It makes a beverage cold
36 "Roses ___ red ..."
37 Raw metal
38 Word after "hair" or "fish"
39 ___ as a fox (sneaky)

32

ACROSS

1 "Every cloud ___ a silver lining"
4 Mr. and ___: Abbreviation
7 Love a whole lot
12 ___ cream cone
13 Paper that describes a debt
14 An actor memorizes them
15 Miles ___ hour (what MPH stands for)
16 Cry loudly
17 Something important that happens
18 ___ on the back (kind of encouragement)
20 Transportation from the airport, sometimes
22 Building that holds tools
24 Cost an ___ and a leg
25 Prefix for "finals" or "colon"
29 Small body of water
30 ___ Schwarz (famous toy store)
31 Country in the Middle East
32 Another name for the Abominable Snowman
33 "That tastes terrible!"
34 Quaker ___ (brand of hot cereal)
35 The words on a page
37 ___ and outs
38 David ___ (rock singer)
41 Ending for "novel" or "guitar"
43 "This ___ job for Superman!": 2 words
46 Pizza topping
47 Suffix for "outrage"
48 "Do ___ disturb"
49 Mary Poppins was one
50 The Atlanta Hawks are in this group: Abbreviation
51 Room where people exercise

DOWN

1 Very cool
2 It's sometimes worth more than a king
3 Snake
4 Light fog
5 Kanga's child in "Winnie-the-Pooh"
6 Type of arithmetic
7 ___ Trebek (the host of "Jeopardy!")
8 Type of arithmetic
9 Eight minus seven
10 ___ and Stimpy (cartoon pals)

11 Ending for "tall" that makes it mean "most tall"

19 Type of arithmetic

21 Run ___ (go wild)

22 "Harriet the ___" (book by Louise Fitzhugh)

23 Tool used in the garden

24 In ___ (in trouble): 2 words

26 Wiping out pencil marks

27 Wrestlers wrestle on it

28 Geniuses have high ones: Abbreviation

36 "___, meeny, miney, mo"

37 "___ small world after all": 2 words

38 "___ voyage!" (what you say to someone going on vacation)

39 "Little Miss Muffet sat ___ tuffet ...": 2 words

40 Be the champ

42 Ship that has a periscope, for short

44 ___ sauce (sauce at Chinese restaurants)

45 Machine that dispenses dollars: Abbreviation

33

ACROSS

1 Experts
5 What one-year-olds learn to do
9 "Wait a ___!" ("Hang on there!")
12 Bum
13 "___ what you mean": 2 words
14 Good buddy
15 Board game where you try to remove items from a body
17 Call ___ day (quit for now): 2 words
18 Bird homes
19 "It ___ my breath away!"
21 Ending for "Vietnam"
22 Questionable
26 Comfortable rooms in houses
27 Board game where you try to find Fame, Happiness, and Money
29 Stated
32 Legendary mountain beast
33 Tiny amount
36 It's added on to a building
38 ___ Prince (Wonder Woman's secret identity)

40 ___ leaves (what Adam and Eve wore)
41 Board game where you try to build a complicated device: 2 words
45 The environment: Prefix
46 "So what ___ is new?"
47 What a dog likes to chew on
48 Color in a rainbow
49 Not sloppy
50 Go to the ___ of the Earth

DOWN

1 Make a call
2 Learn the ___ (find out how things are done)
3 Very fat
4 ___ out (organize)
5 Sense of humor
6 "It's just ___ thought!": 2 words
7 The sign of the Lion
8 Clark ___ (Superman's other name)
9 Dog in "Rugrats Go Wild!"

10 Devoured

11 Cut ___ (be truant)

16 Mongolia is part of this continent

20 "Help wanted" notices

23 Prepare in a pan

24 What something costs

25 "Are we having fun ___?"

27 Letters before F

28 Go by horse

29 More secure

30 "Have ___ day!": 2 words

31 "___ we trust": 2 words

33 The Red ___ (Snoopy's imaginary enemy)

34 ___ out: 2 words

35 Records on a cassette

37 Group that includes Storm and Rogue: Hyphenated

39 "Would ___ too much trouble ...?": 2 words

42 Cheer in Mexico

43 Country near Canada: Abbreviation

44 "On your mark, get ___, go!"

34

ACROSS

1 Tick-___ (clock sound)
5 Not fast
9 Soreness
10 Tree that has needles and cones
11 60 seconds: Abbreviation
14 Pinto or kidney, for example
15 A clarinet player needs one
16 "Are you a man ___ mouse?": 2 words
17 Longitude opposite: Abbreviation
18 What W means, on a compass
19 Character on "South Park"
20 Main course of a meal
22 Go ___ limb (take risks): 3 words
24 Unit of corn
25 Stuff used in making roads
26 ___ snake (small snake)
29 Less chilly
32 Gives a massage
33 "That doesn't sound good": Hyphenated
35 State that borders Idaho: Abbreviation
36 "What am ___ do?": 2 words
37 Smell
38 Heap of sand on a beach
39 Chicken ___ (disease)
40 Tripped
41 "The Adventures of Milo and ___" (movie about a dog and cat)
42 Mr. Flintstone
43 "My country, 'tis of ___ ..."

DOWN

1 Piece of furniture in a kitchen
2 The Pacific ___
3 Very talkative person
4 Barbie's doll friend
5 Shopping ___
6 Doesn't tell the truth
7 "... and ___ grow on" (birthday phrase): 2 words

8 Tuesday follower: Abbreviation

11 Very talkative person

12 Its capital is Teheran

13 The dog in "Peter Pan"

18 "If it ___ up to me ..."

19 It shines in the night sky

21 Rodents

23 State next to Nevada

26 Hold onto

27 Car

28 More impolite

29 ___ Series (baseball event)

30 Bert and ___ ("Sesame Street" friends)

31 ___ Witherspoon (popular actress)

34 Center of a doughnut

37 Go ___ the deep end (lose it)

38 On the ___ (exactly)

35

ACROSS

1 Large
4 Name for a spot on a playing card
7 "___ it!" ("Get out of here!")
11 Hole in ___ (golfing rarity)
12 Christmas ___
13 Ready, willing, and ___
14 Cartoon character from the Stone Age: 2 words
17 Treasure hunters need one
18 Someone who tries to find out secrets
19 Not expensive
22 ___ Angeles
23 Common pet
26 ___ in the dumps (sad)
27 Thing on a shark's back
28 Candy ___ (striped treat)
29 Observe
30 Tic-tac-___
31 Black-and-white bearlike animal
32 Candy ___
33 Relax in a chair
34 Cartoon character from the Space Age: 2 words
40 Largest continent
41 Girl pig
42 Martian's spaceship: Abbreviation
43 It hold pants up
44 Six plus four
45 Kitten's hand

DOWN

1 Nickname for Robert
2 Every once ___ while: 2 words
3 From Berlin
4 Sound from a chick
5 Plant that grows on walls
6 Individual
7 Infant
8 ___ and flow (move like the tide)
9 Once and for ___ (permanently)
10 Peg that a golfer uses
15 Sleep for an hour or so
16 Chin-___ (certain exercises)
19 They contain music: Abbreviation

20 Gardener's tool
21 Female animal on a farm
22 ___ down (get into bed)
23 "You ___ do it!"
24 Peanut butter ___ jelly
25 Brown beverage
27 Large group of trees
28 Red stuff that's put on french fries
30 Game where you try to avoid being touched

31 Hard part of a peach
32 Annoying kid
33 Stitched
34 Talk a lot
35 Suffix for "Siam"
36 ___ and vinegar (salad toppings)
37 Frank's brother, in the Hardy Boys books
38 "Son ___ gun!": 2 words
39 Every ___ and then (once in a while)

36

ACROSS

1 You sip liquid through it
6 Gave a meal to
9 "___ your imagination!"
12 Dried plum
13 "___ not like green eggs and ham!": 2 words
14 Deep-___ diver
15 Competition during a spring holilday: 3 words
18 Performs
19 ___ of a kind (unique)
20 "At ___" ("Relax," in the military)
21 Under lock and ___ (secure)
22 Food fish
23 Woody ___ (famous movie director)
24 She has a day in May
25 "Button your ___" ("Be quiet")
26 ___ situation (case where all the choices are bad): Hyphenated
29 Played the game Sardines
30 Like Garfield the cat
33 "It hit me like ___ of bricks": 2 words
34 Letters that mean "help me!"
35 Stick out like a ___ thumb
36 It's decorated during a winter holiday: 2 words
39 "For ___ a jolly good fellow ..."
40 Digit on the foot
41 Butter ___ (ice cream flavor)
42 Miners dig it up
43 Stick-___ (robberies)
44 Make ___ (be sloppy): 2 words

DOWN

1 Command to a dog
2 Copy an illustration
3 Like metal that's gotten old and wet
4 Have ___ in your pants (be impatient)
5 Very small
6 Demon
7 On the ___ of your seat (very nervous)
8 Grown-up puppy
9 Typical
10 Sight or smell, for example
11 Consumed

1	2	3	4	5		6	7	8		9	10	11
12						13				14		
15					16				17			
18						19				20		
21				22					23			
			24				25					
26	27	28				29				30	31	32
33					34				35			
36			37				38					
39				40				41				
42				43				44				

16 Kitchen, for one
17 Lend a hand
22 Pro and ___ (debate sides)
23 First ___ (Boy Scout merit badge)
24 Prefix with "skirt" or "series"
25 "Mona ___" (famous painting)
26 ___ cheese (Doritos flavor)
27 Go in one ear and out the ___

28 Opposite of "better"
29 Houses
30 Make someone do something
31 Places
32 High school students, for example
34 Come to a halt
35 Flower stalk
37 Disco ___ (character on "The Simpsons")
38 Health ___ (vacation place)

37

ACROSS

1 Use a shovel
4 Person from Iran or Iraq, perhaps
8 Command a dog learns in obedience school
12 "Birds ___ feather flock together": 2 words
13 Part of the face
14 Where a bat lives
15 Very big
17 Tools used by lumberjacks
18 A driver pumps it into a car
19 Paddle for a kayak
21 Very big
24 Very big
28 "Tarzan, the ___ Man"
29 Comes in last place
31 Slippery animal
32 Very big
34 The first man in the Bible
35 What's left after something burns
36 How many shots it's supposed to take, in golf
38 Part of a Halloween costume
41 Very big
46 Feeling of pain
47 Brand of spaghetti sauce
48 Solid ___ rock: 2 words
49 Small golf pegs
50 "X marks the ___"
51 It's put into a car's ignition

DOWN

1 Doberman or Dalmatian, for example
2 "___ Ran the Zoo" (Dr. Seuss book): 2 words
3 It can stop someone from talking
4 Girl's name that reads the same forward and backward
5 Goes bad
6 "___ was going to St. Ives ...": 2 words
7 Turn into
8 Frighten
9 What people pay to the IRS
10 Abbreviation in some addresses
11 It's not "no" or "maybe"
16 "Act your ___ and not your shoe size!"
20 Mornings: Abbreviation
21 Kind of red meat

22 Put ___ brave front (pretend not to be scared): 2 words

23 Precious stone

24 Ending for "fool" or "boy"

25 ___ Flanders (guy on "The Simpsons")

26 "There are plenty of other fish in the ___"

27 Kind of tree

29 ___ Angeles, California

30 "Do unto ___ ..." (the Golden Rule)

33 "Haste ___ waste"

34 Where the elbow is

36 ___ stick (toy you bounce on)

37 Stuck in ___ (doing the same thing over and over): 2 words

38 A gymnast does a routine on it

39 Card without a number or a face on it

40 That lady

42 Siesta

43 Tree with hard wood

44 ___ up (totally finish)

45 "You can ___ that again!"

ACROSS

1 "___ sesame!"
5 ___ Vegas
8 "Don't look ___ like that": 2 words
12 ___ and fortune
13 Part of a fancy stereo system
14 Move back and forth
15 Hostess snack: 2 words
17 ___ and seek
18 "Thanks a ___!"
19 Small brown songbird
21 "What ___ four wheels and flies?"
24 Emergency letters
26 Had a question
29 Ramada ___ (hotel chain)
30 Bit of dust
32 "Where do ___ from here?": 2 words
33 Department ___
35 "Prince ___" (song in "Aladdin")
36 What vain people have a lot of
37 Second ___ (position near the shortstop)
39 Put ___ happy face (grin): 2 words
41 "___ are you talking about?"

43 Hostess snack: Hyphenated
48 A needle has one
49 "___ whillikers!"
50 ___ code
51 Birds that hoot
52 A decade consists of ten of them: Abbreviation
53 The New York ___ (sports team)

DOWN

1 Easy as falling ___ a log
2 ___ for the course (normal)
3 Large bird from Australia
4 ___ Armstrong (the first person to walk on the moon)
5 Portable computer
6 "What ___ doing here?": 2 words
7 Eject, as lava from a volcano
8 They're found in fireplaces after fires
9 Hostess snack
10 Humor magazine
11 It has a lid and lashes
16 Throws

20 Gathering leaves in the yard

21 "Jack fell down and broke ___ crown ..."

22 Snack for an aardvark

23 Hostess snack: 2 words

25 ___ horse (animal you might find near the beach)

27 Silly Putty container

28 Scooby-___ (cartoon dog)

31 People that are identical to other people

34 Gives a grade to

38 Nervous

40 Man who got thrown out of Eden

41 "___ wants to know?"

42 "___ now, brown cow?"

44 Ending for "cash" or "front"

45 State between California and Washington: Abbreviation

46 Part of a tennis court

47 Run out of ___ (lose energy)

ACROSS

1 Cats chase them
5 "What ___ on my summer vacation" (school paper topic, sometimes): 2 words
9 "___ a load of this!"
12 ___ Office (the president's room)
13 Carry along
14 Mail carrier's path: Abbreviation
15 Household animals
16 String on a sneaker
18 Electric ___ (snaky fish)
20 ___ Moines
21 Card game for two people
23 "An apple ___ keeps the doctor away": 2 words
27 "___ that something!" ("How impressive!")
30 Part of the body near the waist
31 Bunches of hay
33 Tool that attacks weeds
34 Leave out
36 It covers the face on Halloween
37 "Pick on someone your ___ size!"
38 Name for a lion
40 Little devil

42 Where you can make your own plate of mixed vegetables: 2 words
47 Not shut
50 "Made in the ___" (phrase on some products)
51 You roll them in Yahtzee
52 Company that makes toy "bricks"
53 February follower: Abbreviation
54 Part of a staircase
55 A ___ in the bucket (small amount)

DOWN

1 It's used to clean a floor
2 "___ never been so insulted in all my life!"
3 Kind of insect
4 "What ___ can I say?"
5 "Virtue is ___ own reward"
6 Play-___ (clay-like material)
7 "How was ___ know?": 2 words
8 Card in Monopoly
9 Kind of insect
10 Abbreviation that makes a list shorter

11 Golf ball's resting place

17 Hawaiian ring of flowers

19 Where a scientist works

21 "Hark! ___ goes there?"

22 Point a camera

24 It blocks a river

25 State in the South: Abbreviation

26 Response that's positive

28 "___ you tell me!"

29 Number of cents in a dime

32 What you might do on the side of a mountain

35 British people drink a lot of it

39 ___ and ends (various things)

41 It grows on old cheese

42 Answer to an addition problem

43 Stubborn ___ mule: 2 words

44 Not the least ___ (not at all)

45 Valuable card in many games

46 George W. Bush's political party: Abbreviation

48 Alter ___ (superhero's non-super identity)

49 Letters after M

40

ACROSS

1 Prefix for "appoint" or "cover"
4 This girl
7 Bakery desserts
12 She was created from Adam's rib
13 ___ of war (game)
14 Stadium
15 Emotion
17 Like the inside of a watermelon
18 Pull hard
19 Big pile
20 In the middle of
22 Kind of transportation
23 What the bride and groom say during a wedding: 2 words
26 Not quiet
27 Floor covering
28 Was sure of
29 Slippery sea creature
30 Spring month
31 The name of a movie or book
32 Word said at the end of a prayer
34 You aren't supposed to do it: Hyphenated

35 Place for travelers to stay for the night
37 Black-and-white bird
40 "You ___ the boss of me!"
41 Large tree
42 Sound a pigeon makes
43 Geeks
44 Organization at a school: Abbreviation
45 House on an island

DOWN

1 Letters before G
2 "So ___ heard"
3 Words said as someone's leaving: 3 words
4 What an angry bee might do
5 Really attractive guy
6 What a chick hatches out of
7 Attaché ___ (things that carry documents)
8 Region
9 Words said as someone's leaving: 3 words
10 Stopping place
11 "I don't know what to ___!"

16 Solid ground
19 Embrace
20 Ginger ___ (type of drink)
21 Bartender on "The Simpsons"
22 Purchase
24 "The First State": Abbreviation
25 "I ___ you one!"
27 Moved really quickly
28 The most valuable piece in chess
30 Thaws
31 Company that makes toy trucks
33 Fix, like torn clothing
34 "Swell!"
35 Grown-up boy
36 Valuable material in a mine
37 Burst a balloon
38 Paper that says how much a person owes
39 "Ready or ___, here I come!"

ANSWERS

1

```
DASH ILL  TIP
OHIO SEA  ONE
HAPPYNEWYEAR
   PAT  YES
SALEM PET  BAT
USED BAR  HAIR
NAG  DRY WEARY
  TOA  TEA
 TRICKORTREAT
 HAM EWE  TACO
 EYE SEE  STEW
```

2

```
PAL  ANTS  BAY
UPA  NAIL  ARE
TEDDYGRAHAMS
   YOO  EVE
ART  ONE ELVIS
DEAR ELM  PACE
SYRUP FAN  NEW
   SET  TEA
NUTTERBUTTER
ONA  LIAR  OWE
WON  SORE  MEX
```

3

```
CATS  HARP
IOWA ELEE  RAG
GREW LIAR  ORE
ATE  APES NAME
RATES NOBODY
 YAKS  NEAR
 OBTAIN SHUTS
THIS MUST  NIP
AIR  GIRL INTO
POD  ALSO MELT
  BEET  PRES
```

4

```
TINA DIG  WARP
IGOR ONE  ISEE
NORTHCAROLINA
   SET  MAT
FAR  MOB TENTS
IGOT RUN  DARE
ROBOT GAB  PAW
   SEA  TUB
MASSACHUSETTS
ERIE HER  AREA
NETS EYE  DYED
```

5

```
BUT  CRY BACON
USE  HOE ADORE
SANDALS  SAWED
 NINE  LIMB
PAINT GAS  OIL
ALSO HEY  HYDE
WAS  OAT ROBOT
 HIPS  POLO
MOOSE MEADOWS
ONEIN ITS  THE
MASTS SET  SOW
```

6

```
RID  BAD  BEE
UFOS EYE  WING
BIGWHEEL  EGGO
  EAT  ARTS
FIBER INA  HEY
ASI BACON  OWE
RAG  ORE DATES
  FORA  AOL
STOW BIGMOUTH
IRON INE  TREE
PIT  AND  EAR
```

7

```
      A D A M   A M A N
O F F   C O L A   D A R E
A L I   T O O T   S K I S
R A N G   M U T E   E S T
S T A L L E D   C L U E S
    L A I D   C H A P
S E E D S   R O O S T E R
T E X   T R A Y   H E R O
A R A B   A D O G   S I P
M I M E   F A T E   T E E
P E S T   T R E E
```

8

```
L A W S   P M S   A S A N
A L I E   E A T   W E R E
D I C E   A M I   E V E R
Y A K   C R A F T   E N D
  S E L L S   F R O N T
  D O E     A N D
  S Q U A T   V I E W S
S T U   R O B I N   A P E
P O E M   W A D   D R A G
A R E A   E S E   O F N O
M E N D   L E O   A S K S
```

9

```
  O A T S   E S S   T O M
  F I R E   L O T   E A R
  F R A N K F U R T E R S
    H Y D E   P A R
A R E   S E W   P A R I S
C O A T   P E P   P E S O
E D D I E   D O C   N A B
  P T A   L O S E
M A R S H M A L L O W S
U S A   E M U   O R E O
D A Y   L O G   R E D S
```

10

```
S I T U P   A P E   A S A
O M A H A   G O D   L O S
W A G O N   E N G L I S H
    H A D   G E E
A M I   M E A   A B L E
S O C I A L S T U D I E S
K E Y S   I N N   T O P
  N B A   T I M
H I S T O R Y   T A L K S
E V E   T E A   E M A I L
Y E T   H A M   D A D D Y
```

11

```
O M I T S   F I B   A L L
C A N O E   O R E   M O O
T R A P E Z E A R T I S T
    S K I   N E W
B I T   S P Y   T I M E D
O D O R   S A W   N A M E
Y O Y O S   M E G   P U N
  O N A   A R K
A N I M A L T R A I N E R
D O C   I S A   S T O V E
D R Y   L O G   S E W E D
```

12

```
A R K   M A T   B A S H
C O O   A R E   E T T E
T W O T I M E S F O U R
  L A D Y   T O M
P E A R   P A R   E B B
A S I   S P A R E   P I E
W E D   A L L   S I G N
  O N A   P R O S
S E V E N P L U S O N E
A G E S   R O D   D O A
W O N T   E W E   E S T
```

13

```
P A S T A   W A S  ▮
U S U A L   A L I   C O T
S I M B A   T I M   O A R
H A M   B E E P   U S A
  ▮ E L M E R   S O N I C
S P R E A D   M O U S S E
T A C O S   T E N S E
A T A   C O R N   L A P
R I M   A X E   V I O L A
T O P   R E N   A R R O W
      A N D   N E S T S
```

14

```
C A P   M A T H   G O A T
O I L   A L I E   A B L E
P R A C T I C E   I S E E
    N O S     O N E
D I E T   C A R D   R I M
O C T   B O X E D   V C R
T E A   O W E D   D A Y S
    R O B     H O T
A S I A   A P R I C O T S
P O U T   R E A D   R O O
E L M S   T A P E   Y E S
```

15

```
S T A Y   P E P   T O P S
O H N O   E A R   O A T H
N E C K   S T I N G R A Y
    H E R O   S E A
M O O S E   D O A   P U T
T U V   A G E N T   I N A
S T Y   G A L   E R R O R
    C A N   A R E A
F L O U N D E R   A N D A
A I N T   E N T   C H O P
T E E S   R D S   H A T E
```

16

```
H O B O   F A W N   P A T
A M A N   E R I E   O L E
G A L S   M E T S   M I N
A H A   V A N   T A M E S
R A N   C L A P   G E N E
    C U R E   R E E L
W H E N   S P I N   H A M
H A B I T   A N D   O R E
A V E   E A S T   B R A T
T E A   E T T E   A S I A
S A M   N E A R   T E L L
```

17

```
D O H   W A D E   T O S S
A N Y   A P E G   I N A N
R T E   S P A G H E T T I
T O N S   E L S E   H I P
  P A N D A S   A M E N
    O W L   T R Y
  B A B E   W A S T E S
A R T   E V I L   H A T S
M E A T B A L L S   S A P
M A L E   S M E E   E G O
O K L A   T A R T   L E T
```

18

```
C A P E   A R M   E T C
A S I A   G O O   L O U
L I T T L E B O P E E P
    Y O O   S N U G
D I M   U S A   P A R T
U N I   T E X A S   N O W
O K R A   E N T   T O O
    A R A B   T O A
J A C K B E N I M B L E
A L L   L E O   P E A S
W E E   E N D   S E P T
```

19

```
M A T S   S O W S   U S A
I N I T   P H E W   K I T
X Y L O P H O N E   U S E
      P I E   T E L L
S A P   T R Y   T E E N Y
I T I S   E A R   G L U E
R A C E D   P O P   E N T
      C A R E   B E A
P R O   A C C O R D I O N
O I L   W H A T   A C R E
E G O   S O N S   M E E T
```

20

```
T A R T   H A S   S W A Y
A S I A   A I M   P A L E
C A M P F I R E G I R L S
        E A R   L E E
B O O S T   C L O S E T S
O W N   M A Y   S O L
B L E N D E R   E M P T Y
      E E L   I T O
W E B E L O S S C O U T S
O W E D   D E N   S P I T
W E D S   Y E T   E A S Y
```

21

```
      J A M S   A B C S
D E S   O B O E   T A R T
I S H   I S L E   A S I A
S P O O N   A S A   K E Y
K N O W   G R A Y   E S S
    T E L E   W E S T
B A H   A N T S   I B E T
E C O   P E R   A T A R I
T H O U   S A N D   L I D
O O P S   I C E D   L E E
N O S E   S E T S
```

22

```
S L E D   D A W N   L A B
P A L E   O H I O   I B E
A C E S   T A N S   G E L
D E C K S     E T H E L
E S T   A P I G   I T T Y
    R I D I C U L E S
S P I N   N E M O   W A S
T I C K S     S M I T H
A L I   L I S A   O T T O
R O T   O V E N   E C H O
S T Y   W E E D   S H E S
```

23

```
F A D   C A P   B U T
A L O T   I N A   O N E
R I C H A R D N I X O N
    E T C   E V E
R A P   E L F   E R R O R
I C E D   E A R   S A F E
M E R I T   T E E   M A D
    S E A   G Y M
R O N A L D R E A G A N
S U E   L I E   Y O Y O
T R Y   S E T   D E W
```

24

```
C H I P   P I G   S A M
A B O U T   R O O   U S A
T O U C H D O W N   N A P
      K E Y   A G E D
S I S   N E W   S N O R E
E D I T   D A M   T W I N
T O T E D   D O I   N O D
    D E E R   A T A
A G O   C O U N T D O W N
N O W   A D S   Y A H O O
T O N   Y E S   M O W S
```

25

```
CAR   DOI   BARON
AGE   OAR   AWARE
TOP   SKI   NAMED
   LIE   STAY
AMAN   THAN   MRS
COCKERSPANIEL
EWE   DUES   ISPY
   DIET   UPS
ABOUT   TIS   ITS
BOONE   EVE   LEO
COPED   RED   EEL
```

26

```
POSED   ALL   SEC
OTHER   LEO   TAR
STOLE   LAW   ARE
SEW   STOPSIGNS
ERN   SOW   VEST
   AYE   CRY
WHAT   SUE   SAN
REDLIGHTS   ICE
IAM   TIE   TIRES
TRI   EVE   EVENT
EST   MET   DENTS
```

27

```
WAG   CAT   SUIT
APE   LIE   ANDI
SUMMERSCHOOL
   SEA   TOA
YAP   ART   PRIDE
ALEG   SIP   ASIA
KAZOO   PUT   MET
   ANT   POT
WINTERSPORTS
ISEE   ACE   AHA
GATE   PIT   YET
```

28

```
WEB   CBS   LAPS
AGO   ALE   AIMAT
GOO   MUNCHKINS
   KNEE   HEE
ISLE   TEA   ALI
THEWIZARDOFOZ
SET   NIP   URGE
   CNN   NOTI
SCARECROW   CUP
EATER   ANN   ASA
CLAW   YES   NET
```

29

```
   CAB   RAFTS
SPA   ALL   AGREE
HIP   RIO   NOONE
OPP   RENT   ODD
RELAY   DONUT
TREMOR   MAPLES
   JANET   SNORT
ALA   DRAT   ONA
DECAY   ASI   PIT
ANKLE   DIE   SEE
MOSES   EAR
```

30

```
SUM   SAP   CRIB
INA   PIE   LATE
ROCKINGHORSE
   NET   USE
MALES   PRE   SEE
OBOE   FAT   CITY
OCT   TAR   DANCE
   MOM   SON
TEETERTOTTER
VANE   AIR   OWE
STUN   MRS   WED
```

31

```
D A B   A D D S   L A C Y
U S A   W O O L   O G R E
D A L L A S C O W B O Y S
    L I K E   W E E
S H O N E   J E T   R U T
H O O K   W A R   L O N E
Y E N   A I R   C O C O A
    A L L   S A C K
M I A M I D O L P H I N S
A C R E   E R I E   E E L
T E E N   R E D S   S T Y
```

32

```
H A S   M R S   A D O R E
I C E   I O U   L I N E S
P E R   S O B   E V E N T
    P A T   T A X I
S H E D   A R M   S E M I
P O N D   F A O   I R A Q
Y E T I   I C K   O A T S
    T E X T   I N S
B O W I E   I S T   I S A
O N I O N   O U S   N O T
N A N N Y   N B A   G Y M
```

33

```
P R O S   W A L K   S E C
H O B O   I S E E   P A L
O P E R A T I O N   I T A
N E S T S     T A K E S
E S E   I F F Y   D E N S
    C A R E E R S
S A I D   Y E T I   B I T
A N N E X     D I A N A
F I G   M O U S E T R A P
E C O   E L S E   B O N E
R E D   N E A T   E N D S
```

34

```
T O C K   S L O W
A C H E   P I N E   M I N
B E A N   R E E D   O R A
L A T   W E S T   S T A N
E N T R E E   O U T O N A
    E A R     T A R
G A R T E R   W A R M E R
R U B S   U H O H   O R E
I T O   O D O R   D U N E
P O X   F E L L   O T I S
      F R E D   T H E E
```

35

```
  B I G   P I P   B E A T
  O N E   E V E   A B L E
  B A R N E Y R U B B L E
    M A P   S P Y
C H E A P   L O S   C A T
D O W N   F I N   C A N E
S E E   T O E   P A N D A
    B A R   S I T
G E O R G E J E T S O N
A S I A   S O W   U F O
B E L T   T E N   P A W
```

36

```
S T R A W   F E D   U S E
P R U N E   I D O   S E A
E A S T E R E G G H U N T
A C T S   O N E   E A S E
K E Y   C O D   A L L E N
    M O M   L I P
N O W I N   H I D   F A T
A T O N   S O S   S O R E
C H R I S T M A S T R E E
H E S   T O E   P E C A N
O R E   U P S   A M E S S
```

37

D	I	G		A	R	A	B		S	T	A	Y
O	F	A		N	O	S	E		C	A	V	E
G	I	G	A	N	T	I	C		A	X	E	S
			G	A	S			O	A	R		
H	U	G	E			I	M	M	E	N	S	E
A	P	E		L	O	S	E	S		E	E	L
M	A	M	M	O	T	H			A	D	A	M
			A	S	H		P	A	R			
M	A	S	K		E	N	O	R	M	O	U	S
A	C	H	E		R	A	G	U		A	S	A
T	E	E	S		S	P	O	T		K	E	Y

38

O	P	E	N		L	A	S		A	T	M	E
F	A	M	E		A	M	P		S	W	A	Y
F	R	U	I	T	P	I	E		H	I	D	E
			L	O	T		W	R	E	N		
H	A	S		S	O	S		A	S	K	E	D
I	N	N		S	P	E	C	K		I	G	O
S	T	O	R	E		A	L	I		E	G	O
		B	A	S	E		O	N	A			
W	H	A	T		D	I	N	G	D	O	N	G
H	O	L	E		G	E	E		A	R	E	A
O	W	L	S		Y	R	S		M	E	T	S

39

M	I	C	E		I	D	I	D		G	E	T
O	V	A	L		T	O	T	E		R	T	E
P	E	T	S		S	H	O	E	L	A	C	E
		E	E	L			D	E	S			
W	A	R		A	D	A	Y		I	S	N	T
H	I	P		B	A	L	E	S		H	O	E
O	M	I	T		M	A	S	K		O	W	N
		L	E	O			I	M	P			
S	A	L	A	D	B	A	R		O	P	E	N
U	S	A		D	I	C	E		L	E	G	O
M	A	R		S	T	E	P		D	R	O	P

40

D	I	S		S	H	E		C	A	K	E	S
E	V	E		T	U	G		A	R	E	N	A
F	E	E	L	I	N	G		S	E	E	D	Y
			Y	A	N	K		H	E	A	P	
A	M	O	N	G		B	U	S		I	D	O
L	O	U	D		R	U	G		K	N	E	W
E	E	L		M	A	Y		T	I	T	L	E
		A	M	E	N		N	O	N	O		
M	O	T	E	L		P	E	N	G	U	I	N
A	R	E	N	T		O	A	K		C	O	O
N	E	R	D	S		P	T	A		H	U	T

ABOUT THE AUTHOR

Trip Payne is a professional puzzlemaker living in Fort Lauderdale, Florida. He made his first puzzles when he was in elementary school, had his first puzzle in a national magazine when he was in junior high, and worked for a major puzzle magazine when he was in college.

He has made kids' puzzles for such places as *Scholastic News*, *Games Junior*, and *TV Guide*. This is his fifth book in the "Crosswords for Kids" series for Sterling Publishing.

Dan Wenke at Bern-Art Studios

WHAT IS MENSA?

Mensa
The High IQ Society

Mensa is the international society for people with a high IQ. We have more than 100,000 members in over 40 countries worldwide.

Anyone with an IQ score in the top two percent of population is eligible to become a member of Mensa—are you the "one in 50" we've been looking for?

Mensa membership offers an excellent range of benefits:
- Networking and social activities nationally and around the world;
- Special Interest Groups (hundreds of chances to pursue your hobbies and interests—from art to zoology!);
- Monthly International Journal, national magazines, and regional newsletters;
- Local meetings—from game challenges to food and drink;
- National and international weekend gatherings and conferences;
- Intellectually stimulating lectures and seminars;
- Access to the worldwide SIGHT network for travelers and hosts.

For more information about American Mensa:
www.us.mensa.org
Telephone:
(800) 66-MENSA
American Mensa Ltd.
1229 Corporate Drive West
Arlington, TX
76006-6103 USA

For more information about British Mensa (UK and Ireland):
www.mensa.org.uk
Telephone:
+44 (0) 1902 772771
E-mail:
enquiries@mensa.org.uk
British Mensa Ltd.
St. John's House
St. John's Square
Wolverhampton
WV2 4AH
United Kingdom

For more information about Mensa International:
www.mensa.org
Mensa International
15 The Ivories
6–8 Northampton Street
Islington, London N1 2HY
United Kingdom